Contents

First edition

Favourite Nursery Rhymes

with illustrations by KEN McKIE

Ladybird Books Loughborough

Little Boy Blue,
Come blow your horn,
The sheep's in the meadow,
The cow's in the corn.
But where is the boy
Who looks after the sheep?
He's under a haycock,
Fast asleep.
Will you wake him?
No, not I,
For if I do,
He's sure to cry.

Three blind mice, see how they run!

They all ran after the farmer's wife;

She cut off their tails
with a carving knife,

Did ever you see such
a thing in your life,

As three blind mice?

Tom, Tom, the piper's son,
Stole a pig and away did run;
The pig was eat
And Tom was beat,
And Tom went howling down
the street.

Simple Simon met a pieman,
Going to the fair,
Says Simple Simon to the pieman,
Let me taste your ware.

Says the pieman to Simple Simon,
Show me first your penny;
Says Simple Simon to the pieman,
Indeed I have not any.

Simple Simon went a-fishing,
For to catch a whale;
All the water he had got
Was in his mother's pail.

Simple Simon went to look
If plums grew on a thistle,
He pricked his finger very much;
Which made poor Simon whistle.

Jack and Jill went up the hill
To fetch a pail of water;
Jack fell down and broke his crown,
And Jill came tumbling after.

Up Jack got, and home did trot,
As fast as he could caper,
He went to bed to mend his head,
With vinegar and brown paper.

Hickory, dickory, dock,
The mouse ran up the clock.
The clock struck one,
The mouse was gone,
Hickory, dickory, dock.

Mary had a little lamb,

Its fleece was white as snow;

And everywhere that Mary went

The lamb was sure to go.

It followed her to school one day,

That was against the rule;

It made the children laugh and play

To see a lamb at school.

Oh! The grand old Duke of York,

He had ten thousand men;

He marched them up
to the top of the hill,

And he marched them down again.

And when they were up they were up,

And when they were down
they were down,

And when they were only half-way up,

They were neither up nor down.

Old Mother Hubbard
Went to the cupboard,
To get her poor dog a bone;
But when she got there
The cupboard was bare
And so the poor dog had none.

Polly put the kettle on,
Polly put the kettle on,
Polly put the kettle on,
  We'll all have some tea.

Sukey take it off again,
Sukey take it off again,
Sukey take it off again,
  They've all gone away.

Wee Willie Winkie
runs through the town,

Upstairs and downstairs
in his nightgown,

Knocking on the window,
crying through the lock,

Are the children all in bed,
it's past eight-o'clock?

Old King Cole
Was a merry old soul,
And a merry old soul was he;
He called for his pipe,
And he called for his bowl,
And he called for his fiddlers three.

Humpty Dumpty sat on a wall,
Humpty Dumpty had a great fall,
All the king's horses,
And all the king's men,
Couldn't put Humpty together again.

*There was an old woman
who lived in a shoe,*

*She had so many children
she didn't know what to do;*

*She gave them some broth
without any bread;*

*Then whipped them all soundly
and sent them to bed.*

Little Miss Muffet
Sat on a tuffet,
Eating her curds and whey;
There came a big spider,
Who sat down beside her
And frightened Miss Muffet away.

Baa, baa, black sheep,
Have you any wool?
Yes, sir, yes, sir,
Three bags full;
One for the master,
And one for the dame,
And one for the little boy
Who lives down the lane.

Sing a song of sixpence,
A pocket full of rye;
Four and twenty blackbirds,
Baked in a pie.

When the pie was opened,
The birds began to sing;
Now wasn't that a dainty dish,
To set before the king?

The king was in his counting-house,
Counting out his money;
The queen was in the parlour,
Eating bread and honey.

The maid was in the garden,
Hanging out the clothes,
When down came a blackbird,
And pecked off her nose.

*Ride a cock-horse
to Banbury Cross,*

*To see a fine lady
upon a white horse;*

*Rings on her fingers
and bells on her toes,*

*She shall have music
wherever she goes.*

What are little boys made of?

Frogs and snails

And puppy-dogs' tails,

That's what little boys are made of.

What are little girls made of?

Sugar and spice

And all that's nice,

That's what little girls are made of.

Ding, dong, bell,
Pussy's in the well.
Who put her in?
Little Johnny Green.
Who pulled her out?
Little Tommy Stout.

What a naughty boy was that,
To try to drown poor pussy cat,
Who never did him any harm,
And killed the mice in his
                    father's barn.

The Queen of Hearts
She made some tarts,
All on a summer's day;
The Knave of Hearts
He stole the tarts,
And took them right away.

The King of Hearts,
Called for the tarts,
And beat the Knave full sore;
The Knave of Hearts
Brought back the tarts,
And vowed he'd steal no more.

There was a crooked man,
 and he walked a crooked mile,

He found a crooked sixpence
 against a crooked stile;

He bought a crooked cat,
 which caught a crooked mouse,

And they all lived together
 in a little crooked house.

*Little Bo-Peep
has lost her sheep,
And doesn't know
where to find them;
Leave them alone
and they'll come home,
Wagging their tails behind them.*

Goosey, goosey gander,
Where shall I wander?
Upstairs and downstairs
And in my lady's chamber.
There I met an old man
Who would not say his prayers,
I took him by the left leg
And threw him down the stairs.

Mary, Mary, quite contrary,
How does your garden grow?
With silver bells and cockle shells
And pretty maids all in a row.

Doctor Foster went to Gloucester

In a shower of rain;

He stepped in a puddle,

Right up to his middle,

And never went there again.

Little Polly Flinders
Sat among the cinders,
Warming her pretty little toes;
Her mother came and caught her,
And whipped her little daughter
For spoiling her nice new clothes.

Hey diddle diddle,

The cat and the fiddle,

The cow jumped over the moon;

The little dog laughed

To see such fun,

And the dish ran away
              with the spoon.